Penmon Point

Penmon Point

POEMS

PETER WALKER

FSC

Published and printed in Wales
on paper from well maintained forests by
Y Lolfa Cyf., Talybont, Ceredigion SY24 5HE
e-mail ylolfa@ylolfa.com
website www.ylolfa.com
tel 01970 832 304
fax 832 782

Penmon Point

(i)

no passing landwards

for the swirling waves
that dip & dart & toss spray high
& lemming-like
rush to hurl themselves
on shingle, shale & slate
hide chiselled reefs
of flinty jagged teeth of barnacle
well-tempered mussel blade
of granite grief
beneath the cloud-grey spume
that snatch at prow
& catch on keel
turn yellow oil-skin sailors
wrapped for rain
to salted cod of corpse

avoid the shallow waters
for in compromise
is still the tolling bell
of broken lives

(ii)

no passing landwards

watch the gull
& echo how (s)he flies
thus as the wind so then the tide
the crest & trough
the pebble-rush drizzle
of the settling foam
the slip & slide & yaw & roll
the blue-black vastness
of a different sky
seeking guidance from
the north that pulls
the west that calls
the ache to find a saffron dawn

no fleshly flotsam now
just fish-picked bones
bleached pebble-white
the spirit feather-flown

After Gwenallt (Duw)

A freely adapted translation of 'Duw' ('God') by D Gwenallt Jones

No yogi, mystic, follower of rules
Who contemplates the navel of his world;
No cloud-wrapped mathematician of the schools
Who solves transcendent problems; nor with curled
And dandied hair all selfish plays for laughs
Or makes the earth a project for his art;
He did not run the show on steely paths
When his creative juices made a start;
He is 'I am', with love within his breast,
This love that is supreme and deep inside,
That flows in waves and waves that know no rest
And wash against the shores of sin and pride;
And then the wave that breaks on Calvary
That carries our redemption on the tree.

Collect

Creator spirit
present in each one of us
in every nook and cranny of your world
fill us with
joy in play
excitement in invention
love in nurture and in care
so that
together
we may play our part
and help heal
the broken heart of this fair place
in the name of
life-giver
child-teacher
and all that binds us
in your holy dance –
thus let it be

Crabbing off Aberdyfi Pier

they go mad for squid
cling five-fold to the linen bag
until
prised apart
they belly-flop into the bucket
small & innocent
crusty & barnacled
pincers big as fathers' thumbs

how many times do they take the bait?
I swear we caught this one
yesterday & the day before

there is no logic to our appetites
the heart goes where it will

daughters
(innocent & worldly-wise)
with fathers, lovers, sons
live & live again
a dream of simple times
when we could grab at our desires
& know that
once the passion had
emptied the air from our lungs
some kind soul
would tip us back into
the murky waters
where we dream again

Credo

if you want me to believe …

then tell me of:

a benevolent creative force
that loves
with the possessiveness of fathers
the selflessness of mothers
& laughs at serendipity
(the word, the concept)
that cries at others' pain
& craves the emulsified unity
of this rainbow world

speak to me of:

one exemplar
humanity writ large
who gives, forgives & gives again
until the gift is given all
& stripes & nails & winding-sheet
are blown away
in the pungent spice of one new dawn

talk to me of:

doves
        that rise & fall & call 'beloved'

flames
>> that leap from lip & heart

rain
>> that builds to tide & sweeps away

tell me of community
>> the gone-before, the still-to-come
speak to me of lives washed clean
>> brought to one-ness
talk to me of evermore
>> today, tomorrow & the days to come

… all this we share …

Funeral Tea

There is the quiet, filling-in of time
(As if a splash of words would waken tears),
And then the coffee-pot and glass of wine,
The sandwiches that loosen jaws and fears;
A chance to shake a hand and share a kiss,
To cup the elbow, steer a face away
And wonder why, at times as sparse as these,
We talk inconsequential yesterdays.
But if relief is palpable and real,
It hides an aching loss – to tell the truth,
We pick upon the scab of how we feel
And suck upon the rancid, hollow tooth
Of grief until the empty space is free …
And thence to home – no 'us' but only 'me'.

Growing Roses

she is in the garden once again
house-coat loose across her geriatric frame
slippered
spectacled
sulphur bulge of knee atop the spindle leg
where once a button held it hid
spidery fingers hold the spray
as she examines each bud of rose
Blessings, Peace, Lichfield Angel
Chaucer, Moonbeam, St Cecilia

she hums a song
recalled from long ago:

let not the aphid mar its beauty
hold back the blackspot
take off the cracked & drooping head
make more room
for this rose in me to bloom …

… despite the sap that sinks
though slow
it surely will yet rise again
just one more summer …
… and one more …
… and yet another one …

Hawkstone Hall – the Trinity

stopped
permanent at five past four
chapel clock hands
insignificant & insignifiable

not noon
pointing God-ward
not 9:15
crucified
not 6 sharp
cutting edge of Holy Spirit
reaching up & out
both north & south

but
… somehow …
hints of all of these

broken clocks
that speak the truth
not once
but twice

but how to know these truths
within this body's broken clock?

above, beside, within
all time is met in this

14

Holy Well

walled by stone
from deep below
in linen chalk
limestone-wrapped

this dribble

ooze of pus on mountain face
lapped by furry tongue of moss
taste of rusty nail & blood
chalybeate & corked bordeaux
bitter hyssop, spittle, death

leaks

until the chalice overflows
& builds
slow … slow … slow …
to cataract of pigeon wing
that dins my ear
with multiplicity of language babble
tumbling phoneme foam
mandarin, xhosa, essex drawl
scally, brummy, hint of cappadocia

& flows

murky ... mingled ... messy ...
into the grateful salty tears
of this waiting presence

Like a Poem by R S Thomas

my first funeral in Wales:

sandbags moved from the weather-bleached door
holding back the autumn storm-rush
that torrents down the curve of road
& threatens a skin-soak of tears

creaking hinges
flaked with rust in a slime of grease
incense of sun-dust & beeswax polish
scented with lavender

a thousand years of hands
have stretched mottled bony fingers
& touched these walls
to raise tired bodies
from the kneel of prayer

the flagstones rutted
with the tramp of feet
at beginnings & endings
& all the in-between
– the bread & cup
– exchange of rings
– blessings & forgiveness
– anointings with a trembling hand

the throats that sing

catch on a falsetto sob of grief
& eke out each verse
chewing long on each long syllable
for the end of singing
marks the beginning
of another song of pain
that has no written score
only the silence
of an empty chair
an empty bed

& then the soft drum
of good damp earth on coffin lid
the feathered rose that falls on pine
the cymbal clash of spade on slate
diminuendo footfall on the flinty path

& all is silence
save the splash of tears
that wash against
the sandbags at the door

One Perfect Sparrow

one perfect sparrow
wearing the benedictine hood of night
waking to the call of cistercian dawn
flew soft into my window
as if the thin veil of glass
between here & eternity
could be shattered
with so gentle a tap

& now his velvet body
cold & still
is but a husk of skin
closed eyes now see within:
the knack of tearing veils
is born in all of us

Prayer

O God save me

let me not be:
a man with a catheter
shuffling along a hospital corridor
carrying a bag of bloody piss

let me not be:
a creature with a black & dusty cough
rattling the fleshless bones
until they crack

let me not be:
a prostrate form dribbling soup and spit
from the only working part
of an inert body
save consciousness

"yet not my will but yours"

I am not Christ enough
to utter words like these
for
I am sore afraid

Remembering – a Funeral on Maundy Thursday

today the sun shone

we did not dip our toe
or dangle ankles
in the spring-cold sea
off safe, bleached jetties
but
ran headlong
into a rising sea of pain
breasting grief
until our feet were caught
and we tumbled
into sea-salt tears

this day and every day:

up and down this fair land of ours
in
cathedral, church and chapel
a choking cleric in a purple stole
seeks to cast a spell
turns back the tide at full
and
let's glimpse sparks of glory
in the pools

today the sun shone

The Mossy Path

the Authorities have pounced –

we have a safety issue:
the mossy path beside the church
will lure the unaware like siren song
endanger life & limb
& leave us responsible
for accidents & acts of God

> fresh-sprung seedling Spring
> shielding ant & aphid
> dimpled resting-place of grasshopper
> cushioned home of spiderling

> dry & cracked in Summer sun
> leeching spores of asthmatic dust
> bleached fawn paragliding gossamer
> downy bed of purring indolence

> dark-green velvet vole of Autumn
> moleskin-smooth
> a Capability lawn
> hiding laurel seed & squirrel treasure-trove

> spongy black of Winter
> or glacier grip of
> crackling icicles
> peat-bog dark & dangerous

thus
dyspraxic youth & aged bent
risk
broken bones
fractured femurs
dislocated digits

then
let us petition
midwives & maternities
picket
mossy wombs
before the seed is sown:

life may lead to accidents
& death
Beware!
you will be liable –
you have been warned

The Parish Priest

a solitary gull
butterflies across the sky

the low spring sun
strikes sparks
off grains of sand
quartz, silica, feldspar, shale
agate, mica, topaz, calcite, garnet
& the rest

I move my head
& different diamonds glow

this is a task:
beneath that singular glance
to let each speck of dust
gleam in the sun
&
conscious of its worth
rejoice & sing –
the infinite variety
made fulsome clear
before it melts to sameness
in the shade

The Penmon Bell

thus time is marked:

the ticking tide
fluttering heart of moon-pull

scimitar sun-slash
from grey-silk dawn to satin

the turning field
that sprouts & swells & crops & fallows

smooth second sweep
circling centrifuge of dreams

the gruel bell above the sea-moan
three thousand times a day
recalls the mask of mist that hides the rock-spear
hints at quicksand current's clawing grasp
states bold that
(unlike tide & sun & field & sweep)
each peal is just an echo
of a peal that is now gone

The Pill-Box

the slow train of the tide
shunting its cargo
back & forth
& back again

a beached whale of a pill-box
slumped & broken
after winter storms
its look-out eyes
cataracted with sand
& a God-handful of pebbles

& behind
forty miles & a million lifetimes away
saddle-back silhouette of Eryri
calling with that constant voice
that whispers from
glacial valley
to eagle's nest

on my cheek
a breath of breeze
now warm now cool
each breath
a different breath
distinct & individual
breathing with the rhythm
of the same free heart

from mountain-top to shore
that self-same beat
eroding
concrete into pliant sand
pill-box into powdered shell
transience into eternity

Transfiguration

'shall we make three booths?'

a horny hand stops us
mid-gather
sun-leathered hands a-grasp
with reed & leaf & clump of grass

this was no miracle
just a touch of sun
that haloes heads
& screws the eyes up tight
that leads to visions
& fires the mind
with wild imaginings
of a revolutionary kind

just wait …

as bare-bone winter trees
retain the seed of life
so tombs a-rustle
with a 'yet I am'

the true transfiguration
does not stand
on mountaintops & shout
but
is a quiet stirring

& a moved stone
an empty chrysalis
in a pale-blue Easter morn

Two Memorials

letters
beaten by snow, frost, rain
creeping lichen
butterbur
illegible
cracked & mossy
headstones at impossible angles
grave-back bent & bowed
one false foot will touch dusty bone
this caught moment
stone-trapped
as if fragile slate
can live forever

sheltered by the warmth of candles
deftly chiselled by a mason's art
finished with curlicues
crisp & precise
seeking to buy eternity
fenced off & neat
distinct
displaying pomp & titles

& in the end
names eroded from stone
are as impermanent
as names in unremembered genealogies

but
lives are cherished
by a bigger heart
that carves the names
in love

We are TV

"the vicar is here –
to talk about the funeral"

I incline my head to show concern
shake hands
say the well-rehearsed & well-used words

in reverence & respect
the sound is dimmed a notch
a glance to me
the eyes flicker to the screen
back & forth
back & forth

"this was his favourite –
it's what he would have wanted –
to go on as if nothing had changed"

as if the proof of eternity
were an endless loop of re-runs
on evermore remote satellite channels
run by God-TV
where characters repeat well-crafted lines
& laughter (always canned)
gives us the cue
& we ignore
the alcohol, divorce & tabloid sleaze
cancer, car-crash, therapy

that got them in the end
as if the future can be pushed back
like a wayward lock of hair
in last-century style

but somehow, somewhere
when the licence has expired
or the pixels freeze
or the remote
       its numbers illegible through rubbed-finger use
gives up the ghost
or the picture breaks
& goes black one final time
then
maybe
you will see that life
like a pilot no-one watched
will be cancelled

Welsh Beach – looking west

strange light

this beached medusa
gob of mucus
turquoise, is it? translucent green? limpid blue?
reflecting back grey ocean
tidal flow, west to east
flecked horses riding high
whips of mane against the face
crayoned light on the horizon
a world reversed

here be monsters
come to wash clean
the detritus of a different tide:
  – a gull that once
    scribbled white wings against a coal-black sky
    now its half-picked flesh stinks rotten
  – plastic bottles, yellowed but eternal
    they will not die
  – dried sea-wrack, cracking underfoot
    once slimy smooth

strange light

I see coracles
storm-tossed, ascetic bards
seeking … seeking …

34

"It is only half-written," they say
"Write on … an 'i' of body on a beach at dawn …
… a 'v' of kite waiting on its prey …
… an 'o' of gasping mouths in love …
… a 't' of agony …
… an alphabet we must yet write."

strange light

The Feast of St Thomas

there was a time
when dreaming was the only certainty
when myriad signposts
stood stark & sluttish in wanton invitation
against a sun-burst blaze of possibility

but now I prod the wound of might have been
& poke the purple scar of causes lost

is this the way it was in that still room?
is this how it was ever meant to be?

to touch the absence that hung limp like flesh
pinned only by the screaming nails of faith
until even they were loosed
& bloodied we were borne away
to float upon the darkness of the sea
& in that fragile buoyancy
to feel the dreaming start again

Summer

today:
the heat is silver paper in my teeth
Bedlam furnace spills hot iron again
& sulphur wraiths burn nostril hair

the haze hangs condensation
on horizon's washing-line
& pegs the dripping bodies
limp

my own flesh scorches at my touch

I swear the roses sweat sweet sugar
paddled by gangly aphids
whose swollen bellies
pregnant with sap
are eyed with soporific languor
by creaking carapace of predator

and then:
one, two, three
gobs of God-spit
sandy-brown
hawked from throat of pollen & threshing dust
slap like swimmers' soles
on slab & slate

and more:

a thousand tippy-toes of dancers' feet
on feather fern & nettle leaf
make them *plié* in a ballerina bow

and now:
the ebb & flow applause of rain
atavistic memory of monsoon
thunderclap 'Bravo!'
& strobe of lightning
catching a snapshot of this one fair day
that words seek to hold
to taste again
as though the belch of memory
were a guarantee of resurrection

Confession

the neighbours look askance at me

purple thrift
tendrils of buttercup
cotton clocks of dandelion
daisies
a runner from an errant strawberry plant
cups of clover and a hint of mint
camomile sage and lemon thyme

"If I were you," they say,
"I'd give that lawn some
serious attention …
weed out those interlopers
and feed richly …
it won't take long …
soon you'll have
a bowling green …"

cossetted
striped
ordered

image of a perfect life
bordered with a buttoned jacket of self-control

but

let me walk upon my meadow
sweet scent of rosemary and oregano

let me feel beneath my toes
a thistle prickle and a crack of sap

let me see amongst the green
red campion and gold nasturtium head

let me embrace
the fullness of our blue earth

closest to the aching heart of God

Above Penhelig

a view glimpsed through trees
scared stickle fingers
another winter's bare-black bones:

grey shot silk shimmer
fluorescent ripple meander
merging in a foamy kiss with slow-ebbing tide

pale horses intertwine:
pursed salt with sweet fern berries
old ivory dawn with bracken brown
demerara yeast of spume

pike & whiting
embrace in salmon-skin

beneath the speckled sunhaze
dichotomy is the construct
of a fevered mind
anthropomorphic hierarchs
longing for redemption

and then:

swoop of kite
forked fantail
rainbowing over water

Four Psalms

Psalm 19

The skies reveal the glory of the Lord;
They speak, as eloquent as any sage
With rich vocabulary; every word
Attests throughout the world from age to age.
The sun rides out, a knight in rich array,
From east to west the bridegroom makes a show.
The Law of God is perfect; every day
Revives, enlivens, makes the heart to glow.
This Law is pure, and precious as the gold
That drips its honey-sweetness from the comb.
Thus comes reward: to do as God has told.
God, see my errors! Welcome me back home!
Keep me from sin! And may my thoughts and voice
Be pleasing to you – then I can rejoice!

Psalm 27

When I am castled in the Lord's good heart
No siege of evil men can bring me down.
I ask just this, that I may never part
From you, but seek you in your temple grounds.
I shall be safe, protected, lifted high,
Will sing with joy, my enemies disgraced.
So hear me when I call and answer my
Requests for mercy; I will seek your face –
Oh, do not hide, reject or turn away!
You are my Saviour, make my path be straight
And let me learn the markers on the way.
Defend me when they breathe the fires of hate.
But wait I must: the Lord will sow the land
With seeds of goodness from his patient hand.

Psalm 48

The city of our Lord demands we praise
Him – high and beautiful as Everest.
Within her walls, the Lord himself will raise
To keep and hold her tight unto his breast.
The forces round about have fled in pain
And fear as when a child is born to light;
Their frigates, storm-tossed, cannot sail again,
And God secures the locks that keep her tight.
Within these temple walls we think of your
Unfailing love, ubiquitous in power.
All Zion sings in praise of your good Law.
I measure walls and count up every tower,
View ramparts that for evermore will stand
As witness to the guiding of your hand.

Psalm 148

Praise God within the starry heights above,
Praise God, you rains that tumble from the cloud.
Praise God, you angel hosts, sing of your love,
Praise God, you sun and moon – stars, shout out loud!
Praise God, for he commands – all comes to be.
Praise God, he will sustain throughout all time.
Praise God, you fish and creatures of the deep.
'Let us praise, too!' say mountain-ash and pine.
'Let us!' say hill and cedar, storm and snow.
'Let us!' say prince and government and king.
'Let us!' say eagle, robin, bat and crow.
'Let us!' says every nation, 'Let us sing!
Let us exalt his name, his name alone!
Praise God, he holds us near and brings us home!'

Gloria

So Father, Son and Holy Spirit free
Be ever glorified. Thus let it be.

The Vicar's got Tourette's

so love your ** neighbour
with all your ** heart
just learn this ** lesson
& then we'll ** start
to build the ** Kingdom
& put the world to right
restore the broken-hearted
& shine Christ's ** light
bring down the ** mighty
& lift the ** down
redeem creation's glory
& Christ will wear the crown
so don't just ** listen
get on your ** feet
& do what Christ has asked of you
in every ** street

This book is just one of a whole range of
Welsh interest publications from Y Lolfa.
For a full list of books currently in print,
simply surf into our website

www.ylolfa.com

for secure on-line searching and ordering.

TALYBONT CEREDIGION CYMRU SY24 5HE
website www.ylolfa.com
e-mail ylolfa@ylolfa.com
tel (01970) 832 304